Managing
Difficult Interactions

Pocket Mentor Series

The *Pocket Mentor* Series offers immediate solutions to common challenges managers face on the job every day. Each book in the series is packed with handy tools, self-tests, and real-life examples to help you identify your strengths and weaknesses and hone critical skills. Whether you're at your desk, in a meeting, or on the road, these portable guides enable you to tackle the daily demands of your work with greater speed, savvy, and effectiveness.

Books in the series:

Managing Difficult Interactions

Expert Solutions to Everyday Challenges

Harvard Business Press

Boston, Massachusetts

Copyright 2008 Harvard Business School Publishing Corporation

Printed in the United States of America

12 11 10 09 08   5 4 3 2 1

Library of Congress Cataloging-in-Publication Data

Managing difficult interactions : expert solutions to everyday challenges.
    p. cm. — (Pocket mentor series)
  Includes bibliographical references.
  ISBN 978-1-4221-2508-3
  1. Conflict management. 2. Interpersonal confrontation. 3. Interpersonal conflict.
4. Interpersonal communication. 5. Interpersonal relations. I. Harvard Business
School. Press.
  HD42.M364 2008
  658.4'053—dc22

                                              2008022311

The paper used in this publication meets the requirements of the American National Standard for Permanence of Paper for Publications and Documents in Libraries and Archives Z39.48-1992.

Contents

To Learn More   77

Further titles of articles and books if you want to go more deeply into the topic.

Sources for Managing Difficult Interactions   83

Notes   85

For you to use as ideas come to mind.

Mentor's Message: Why Learn How to Manage Difficult Interactions?

Finding yourself in a prickly exchange or conversation is one of the *unpleasant surprises* of daily life in the workplace—whether it's with your boss, a peer, an employee, or even a customer or supplier. We're inclined to avoid these difficult interactions, just as we're inclined to avoid other discomforts. And why not? Difficult interactions catalyze negative feelings such as frustration, annoyance, and anger. At those moments, our needs for safety, understanding, and effectiveness—among others—aren't being met. But ignoring these exchanges often makes things worse. Unattended hostility and hurt—key features of a confrontation—can sap your energy, reduce team productivity, and ruin a workplace relationship.

Misunderstanding and conflict are part of the fabric of human interaction. Situations that include them are opportunities for the players to learn more about themselves, each other, and what it takes to get work done in a collaborative fashion.

It's almost always possible to turn a tough interpersonal exchange around—and even strengthen a relationship in the process. That might sound like a pipedream. However, we are social beings after all. We want to get along, to live and let live. When we're in touch with our nobler aspirations, we even want to help others. Yes, we really do!

Learning to navigate your way through difficult interactions takes some self-awareness and skill. It also takes courage. Getting good at facilitating the conversation—from conflict to connection—takes practice. This book shows you how.

In the pages that follow, you'll discover what causes difficult interactions and how to face the barriers that prevent many managers from dealing with them. You'll also learn practical techniques for determining which conflicts merit your attention, for assessing what's *really* going on in a difficult interaction, and for managing the emotions that often arise in such situations. Additional sections outline strategies for solving the problem behind a conflict and for reconciling differences among your employees.

I hope you find this book useful. Good luck on your expedition.

Barry Rosen, Mentor

Barry Rosen is a board member and past president of Interaction Associates (IA). Responsible for the development of many of Interaction Associates' best-selling learning programs, including Facilitative Leadership and Essential Facilitation, Mr. Rosen has coached leaders and trained consultants in teamwork and collaboration skills since 1980. Interaction Associates, Inc. is a performance-improvement company that equips clients with collaborative strategies to solve problems and realize opportunities. Since 1969, Interaction Associates has helped global leaders, the *Fortune* 100, and government agencies to overcome their most difficult collaborative challenges.

Managing Difficult Interactions: The Basics

What Are Difficult Interactions?

WORKPLACE INTERACTIONS AREN'T always easy. Everybody knows that. In fact, most human interactions—however transactional and routine—include some measure of uncertainty and wonder. That's because we human beings do things not simply by instinct, but by choice. At choice points, we consider, however quickly and subconsciously, several variables. What do I want? Is there a threat? Do I trust the person I'm interacting with? What's the quickest way to get what I want? And so forth.

Difficult interactions are those exchanges with other humans beings where the questions we're asking ourselves don't have quick answers. We experience uncertainty. Our uncertainty leads to a feeling of fear. We intuit that we may not be able to meet a need, and we enter a zone called threat. The Threat Zone.

Dealing effectively with our sense of threat and the difficult interaction occurring between ourselves and others is both an "inside job" and an "outside job."

The inside job is about noticing and managing our automatic thoughts and feelings. It's about slowing down and remembering that we deserve to have our needs met. The outside job is about treating the other person with respect and courtesy, and applying a few practical techniques for solving the problem (or simply completing a transaction) in a collaborative fashion.

Examples of difficult interactions

Let's further our understanding of difficult interactions and how to make the best of a challenging situation, by asking and answering three questions:

- What does a difficult interaction look and feel like?

- Why do managers tend to avoid dealing with these difficult interactions directly?

- How can we address the barriers—internal and external—to dealing with them?

You're arguing with a peer because you think he consistently shoots down your ideas. Two of your employees routinely attack each other verbally during meetings. Your boss makes sarcastic remarks to you and other managers. A customer regularly makes unreasonable demands on your team.

These are all difficult interactions. They have a few things in common: people are disagreeing, either directly or implicitly by their actions. At the moment, the resulting conflict may appear impossible to reconcile. You, as either a participant or an observer, feel stuck between two equally bad alternatives.

If you don't deal with the situation, it may escalate to highly undesirable outcomes—including strained relationships, wasted time, and poor performance. If you do deal with it, the situation may escalate into even greater conflict, entrenched positions, and a major diversion of your attention.

As you may have noticed in the above examples, difficult interactions can arise between any two individuals: supervisor and direct report, two peers, or several members of a department or team. When such situations crop up between two of your direct reports—for example, several team members argue repeatedly over who's responsible for what tasks, or one employee accuses another of not being committed to a project—you need to take action quickly. Otherwise, your team's productivity may suffer.

Removing barriers to dealing with conflict

The table "Typical barriers to dealing with difficult interactions" lists several potential barriers and suggests a proactive approach for removing each type.

The price of admission to effective management is your willingness to tackle confrontations head-on. Despite the challenge, it's part of your job to recognize situations in which people's needs aren't being meet, and the results are conflict and alienation. If you don't do it, who will? A pattern of disagreements will undermine workplace relationships, eat away at motivation, and damage performance in your team or work group.

"I always prefer to believe the best in everybody—it saves so much time."
    —Rudyard Kipling

Typical barriers to dealing with difficult interactions

Barrier	Proactive approach
Fear of interpersonal conflict	Acknowledge that although conflict can be uncomfortable, it's a fact of life. Focus on the positive outcomes of addressing conflict.
Failure to recognize that you have a problem with another person in the workplace	Notice the quality of your workplace relationships. Ask which relationships seem tense, frustrating, or unproductive. Consider acknowledging that these relationships are hampered by difficult interactions.
The belief that a difficult interaction is the fault of others	Acknowledge your role in the difficulty. Identify what you can do to improve the situation.
The conviction that other people won't change, even if you try to improve the situation	Remind yourself that you're not trying to change another person. Rather, you want to alter the way the two of you interact. You can do that by changing your own behavior.
The desire to accept the status quo because you're not prepared to manage the outcome of the situation	Evaluate whether the risks of the difficult interaction are worth the benefits of an improved situation. If they are, map out a plan and carry it out.
The belief that the problem will resolve itself	Remind yourself that most problems don't resolve themselves.

Understanding that improvement is possible

Though managing conflicts is challenging, the rewards are well worth the effort.

- Difficult interactions become easier to handle.

- You prevent these situations from escalating into crises.

- You engage in more productive interactions.

- You feel greater freedom to take action in tough situations, as well as a stronger sense of self-respect.

- You strengthen your workplace relationships.

Managing difficult interactions requires intention and attention. But you *can* master this important managerial responsibility. Some things on which to focus are:

- Which difficult interactions require prevention or intervention? Which can I ignore or defer?

- What are the facts of the situation?

- What feelings are people expressing? What needs do people have that aren't being met?

- How are people—through their words or actions—getting in the way of helping others meet some need?

- What are some options for solving the problem so that everyone's needs can be met in some important way?

What Causes Difficult Interactions?

IFFICULT INTERACTIONS tend to stem from differences between people—in their positions and interests; in their perceptions, motivations, and styles; and in their life experiences and cultural backgrounds. By understanding the role of these types of differences in interpersonal conflict in the workplace, you position yourself to begin dealing with them productively.

Differences in positions and interests

Often, conflicts arise when two people have different *positions* (stances) and *interests* (desires) at stake concerning a particular *issue*.

Consider the following example, in which the issue at hand involves vacation time.

You oversee several teams, each of which has a leader. Randall, a team leader who's relatively new to the company, comes to you and complains about having less vacation time than the other team leaders. On this issue of vacation time, you and Randall have differences, as shown in the table "Different positions and interests."

When two people go head-to-head over different positions or interests, tension and conflict can intensify. The more you can focus a difficult interaction on interests, the more likely it is that you can find a creative solution that at least partially satisfies both people's interests. In the example above, you could propose to Randall that he take one more week of vacation but that he use the

Different positions and interests

	Randall's	Yours
Position (stance)	"I should receive the same amount of vacation as the other team leaders."	"You can have the same amount of vacation when you have been here longer."
Interest (desire)	"I want to be treated fairly."	"I need you to be around to manage this large software implementation."

time as a series of long weekends rather than five contiguous days. That way, he knows he's being treated fairly, and you ensure that he's not away from the project for too long.

Differences in perceptions, motivations, and styles

In addition to differences in positions and interests on a particular issue, other kinds of differences can spawn difficult interactions. The table "Different perceptions, motivations, and styles," shown on page 13, provides examples.

Differences in life experiences and cultural backgrounds

Differences in two people's cultural backgrounds, educational and professional experiences, gender, age, and race can also create

What Would YOU Do?

The Trouble with Terry

BRAD DOESN'T KNOW exactly when it will happen, but someday Terry is going to drive him over the edge. She spends hours reworking even the most routine tasks—and is sometimes late with a deliverable, which in turn affects Brad's scheduling. Also, she tends to take a critical look at group decisions—sometimes causing the group to revisit decisions already made. Still, Brad knows that when Terry takes on a complicated or difficult project, she will be thorough, intelligent, and persistent. Brad sees that Terry's hard work and critical attention to detail have made valuable contributions to the group, but Terry's careful approach clearly has an adverse effect on him. He is beginning to avoid her—and he senses she may be avoiding him. How can he approach Terry? Or should he approach her at all? He wouldn't be able to change her anyway . . .

What would YOU do? The mentors will suggest a solution in *What You COULD Do.*

---

misunderstandings and tensions in the workplace. The totality of each person's life experiences influences his or her assumptions about how the world should work and what can reasonably be expected from others.

Different perceptions, motivations, and styles

Difference	Example
Perceptions about what's critical	You view management's directives as more important than a team member does.
Motivations and intentions	You are motivated by quality, while a colleague is motivated by personal achievement.
Work style	You like to put all issues on the table at once, but your supervisor prefers to grapple with problems one at a time.
Communication style	You prefer to be updated about problems through written communication, while an employee finds it easier to update you by dropping by for an informal conversation.

"A great many people think they are thinking when they are merely rearranging their prejudices."

—William James

When two individuals come from vastly different backgrounds and experiences, difficult interactions can arise over just about any situation in the workplace. Consider the following example:

Stella is a sixty-one-year-old manager in charge of a Web site development project. As the project unfolds, she begins to get a vague sense that some of her team members don't give enough consideration to her suggestions for managing the project. One day, she overhears one younger team member say to another, "You can't expect a near retiree to really understand the Web." In this case, age differences may have caused the younger team members to assume that because of her age, Stella is incapable of managing a Web project effectively. Thus, the team members don't fully accept her leadership or value the knowledge she brings to the project.

Unless she addresses this difficult situation, Stella is likely to have problems leading her project team effectively.

Tip: To mitigate the tension that can arise during difficult interactions, try playing up similarities (in interests, background, and so forth) and match the other person's gestures, body posture, and speaking style. Feelings of empathy and connection lead to higher comfort levels and rapport.

What You COULD Do.

Remember Brad's problem with Terry and his uncertainty about how to handle it?

Here's what the mentor suggests:

If Brad is beginning to avoid Terry, it's time to sit down and talk with her. While Brad has a clear picture of what he thinks the problems are, he should find out how Terry perceives the situation. It's possible she sees things quite differently.

For example, perhaps her rework ultimately saves time. Or maybe she revisits group decisions because she thinks they are rushed and not carefully considered. Once Brad understands Terry's point of view and gets to the root cause of the situation, he can then move toward resolving their differences and improving their interactions. His goal should be not to change her, but to change how they interact—which may mean changing his own behavior.

Deciding Which Difficult Interactions to Address

MANAGING DIFFICULT INTERACTIONS takes time, patience, and energy. Thus, before you plunge into trying to address a tough situation with someone, it's useful to carefully consider several factors. Your primary aim is to invest your time and energy wisely—in situations that have the best chance of being improved.

For conflicts that you've decided are worth tackling, it's useful to apply techniques for (1) getting at the facts behind the situation, (2) understanding the emotions involved, (3) dealing with concerns about self-image that often accompany such situations, and (4) coming up with solutions to the problem. All of these steps are discussed at length in later sections of this book.

But first, let's talk about how to determine which prickly situations you should deal with—and which you should let go.

Determining whether you're part of the problem

Sometimes conflicts with another person stem more from what's going on inside you than from what's going on between you and the other person. In such instances, a discussion about the interaction may not yield any benefits.

For example, suppose you keep taking on several of your direct reports' problems rather than helping them learn how to solve them on their own. You find yourself working more and more overtime, and your real managerial work stacks up. You begin experiencing stress-related problems and feeling resentful toward these employees.

Are these difficult interactions that would benefit from a frank discussion? Perhaps not—if the reason you keep taking on direct reports' problems is that you fear being seen as incompetent or uncaring when you hand problems back to their rightful owners.

Instead of a lengthy, tense, and time-consuming discussion with your employees, you could instead honestly examine the motives behind your urge to solve employees' problems. And you could remind yourself of the importance of delegating as a managerial skill. In this case, changing your own attitudes and behaviors regarding delegating would probably improve your relationships with your employees far more than talking about the situation would. And it would take less time and energy.

Examining your motives

With some disagreements, you may feel tempted to simply let loose with your emotions. "After all," you might think to yourself, "at least I'm doing *something* to deal with the situation." But before you vent, ask yourself whether you're really just seeking short-term emotional relief instead of doing what's best for the long run.

Dumping your negative feelings on someone who irritates you may get you some temporary relief and even prompt the person to change his or her ways . . . for a while. But you may have also done so much damage in the process of venting that the relationship is frayed for the long run.

Identifying important relationships

It's a good idea to aim for positive working relationships with everyone you work with. Dare I say it, however: some workplace relationships are more important than others. In deciding whether to deal with a difficult interaction, consider *how important* your relationship with that person is. Also consider *whether the relationship is long term or short term* and *how high the stakes are*. For example:

- **An important relationship.** You're having difficulty working with Carl, your supervisor's assistant, because of differing work styles. You interact with him daily on critical matters. That relationship has high priority. You will probably want to find ways to deal with the conflicts that arise between you and Carl.

- **A not-so-important relationship.** You can't seem to build a shared understanding with Toni, another member of a short-term project you're working on. You may decide not to invest the time and energy required to improve the relationship. After all, once the project is over, you probably won't be working closely with Toni again on such a high-stakes effort.

Gauging the chances of improvement

Suppose you're having prickly interactions with someone who seems troubled emotionally or has a history of conflict-laden relationships with people across a wide range of situations. For example:

- Your new supervisor has a hair-trigger temper, and you've learned that all of your predecessors have left the company within three months of starting their jobs.

- An employee has a sarcastic sense of humor and repeatedly puts others down, no matter how often you try moving her to different teams.

- A colleague has let long-standing personal problems undermine his performance on the job (including collaboration with peers on cross-functional projects) and has shown no willingness to get help.

In these cases, there's little chance that your intervention will improve the situation in a sustainable way. Instead, you may want to consider a different course of action. For instance, to mitigate the conflict with an ill-tempered new boss, you might try arranging to report to someone else in the organization. If that fails, you might consider leaving the company and finding a work situation where your boss is actually committed to your success. If you don't want to leave your job, recognize that the situation may be beyond your ability or responsibility to address by yourself. Consider getting help from human resources or other professionals in your company who are charged with resolving such situations.

When feedback doesn't change the behavior of an employee who insists on using hurtful humor, a formal reprimand is in order; then disciplinary action, and finally dismissal. If you select a formal disciplinary course of action, make sure you follow company personnel policies.

With the colleague who's not pulling his weight on a project because of personal problems, you may want to find ways to avoid working on projects with him. Another approach is to request that the team leader or sponsor review prospective team members' complementary skills and potential challenges, so that potential conflict can surface before the project begins. Finally, ask your own supervisor to help you stay off that team.

A version of the serenity prayer is a good reminder in these cases: Lord, give me the grace to accept the things that I cannot change, the courage to change the things I can change, and the wisdom to know the difference.

Tip: If you've decided not to resolve a conflict with a particular person, remind yourself that letting go of a difficult situation doesn't mean you're an uncaring person.

Whatever criteria you use for deciding whether to confront someone about a disagreement between the two of you, remember that you can't force someone to change his or her attitudes or behaviors. All you can do is try to improve the relationship by changing the way *you* behave and the way you and the other person interact.

Step 1: Assessing the Facts

S O, YOU'VE IDENTIFIED a conflict situation that you believe merits an intervention. The first step is to assess the
facts. In any difficult interaction, the two people involved see the
facts of the situation from unique angles. To begin to resolve a
particular conflict, you need to explore these facts through frank
discussion.

You're probably familiar with the maxim that says there are two
sides to every story. The same is true for disagreements in the
workplace: Each person involved views the situation according to
a specific set of facts that are important for him or her.

To lay the groundwork for resolving a problem, each person
should learn the facts—and perception of fact—that are influencing the other person's position. That takes communication. The
guidelines introduced in this section can help.

Sharing perceptions of what's going on

Terry reports to Brad. Suppose that she keeps submitting project
reports late even though Brad has repeatedly complained and in-
sisted that Terry complete the reports on time. But the more Brad
complains and insists, the more annoyed Terry gets.

To get at the facts, Brad and Terry should try explaining their
sides of the story, including the situation's impact on them. For example, Brad could say, "When you send in reports late, I end up

doing a lot of extra work to compensate. I have to spend two hours filling out paperwork myself. I also have to explain to the other team members that the information they need will be coming late. That throws the whole project behind schedule."

Terry, then, might say, "I've been really stressed out lately, because I've had a bunch of new prototypes to evaluate, and they've all had problems. I couldn't seem to get to the project reports. When you continually complain about the late reports, I get the impression that you don't care about how well the prototypes are handled."

The next step is for Brad to stop and think about what may have caused him to see the situation as he does. He could consider information he's gathered in the past, previous experiences, and assumptions about what's important. Then he could share this information with Terry and ask her to do the same. Brad could share his previous experiences.

For example, he could say, "The last time I led a project of this complexity, we had real problems during implementation after we stopped circulating weekly updates to everyone." He could then share information with Terry by adding, "This worries me, because I recently read an article saying that poor team communication is often the cause behind failed projects." Finally, Brad might share his assumptions about what is important. "In my view, we don't stand a chance of breaking into the new market we've identified unless we can successfully carry out our projects."

Terry, in reciprocating, could also share information, previous experiences, and her assumptions about what is important. For example, she might say, "The latest speech by our CEO made me realize that we've got to accelerate the product prototyping process.

I've learned from last year's projects that when you have to make a choice between filling out paperwork and getting the actual work done, it's better to focus on the work. The paperwork can always be done later."

By sharing the information, experiences, and assumptions behind your view of the difficult situation, you and the other person begin understanding each other—a step that's essential to resolving problems.

Discovering intentions

If you sense a threat or conflict arising, take a moment to regain your composure. Then clarify with the other person what your intentions have been during the difficult exchanges you've had together. Consider this exchange between Brad and Terry:

> **Brad:** I've been trying to make sure that everyone on the project team gets the information they need to handle the tasks they're accountable for, on time. That's the only way we can keep the overall project on schedule.

> **Terry:** I figured that by focusing on accelerating the prototyping process, we could prevent bottlenecking in the early stages of the product-development cycle. If the process gets held up in the beginning of the cycle, the rest of the cycle is going to be in trouble too—and the whole thing will end up delayed.

When you compare intentions, you may (as in this case between Brad and Terry) discover that you both have similar aims and priorities. At the very least, you may realize that each of you has perfectly admirable intentions, even if they differ. In either case, you each will probably conclude that the other person isn't deliberately trying to make life difficult!

Acknowledging contributions to the problem

Most conflicts aren't caused by one person. Both parties have played some part in creating the situation. To create a sense of ownership for resolving the issue, honestly acknowledge what you've done to contribute to the problem. Ask the other person to do the same. Let's see how Brad and Terry handled this:

Brad: I think that by constantly complaining about late reports, I gave you the impression that I didn't care about the prototyping process.

Terry: I can see that by letting the project updates slip, I caused you to question whether the project overall would stay on schedule.

Step 2: Addressing the Emotions

I N T H E P R O C E S S of uncovering the facts, you'll want to also pay attention to the feelings behind the difficult situation. As you probably have noticed, difficult interactions trigger powerful emotions in the people involved. Those feelings may differ from person to person—even in the same situation.

Basic feelings are sad, glad, mad, afraid—and variations on those four. Positive feelings generally mean that needs are being met. For instance, we feel joy when we've completed a difficult assignment successfully. We have troubled feelings when our needs aren't being met. For example, we may feel resentful when a colleague doesn't complete an assignment after we've worked half the night.

In a difficult situation, it's useful to identify and name the feelings you're experiencing. If feelings are ignored or suppressed during a difficult interaction, they can come out in other ways—such as body posture, facial expressions, and long pauses. They can also make it hard for the participants to listen to one another. If such emotions become extremely intense, the people involved may simply avoid each other, because the unresolved feelings seem so threatening.

Addressing emotions involves more than just venting. How does one identify and share one's feelings during a difficult interaction without blaming the other person or increasing your sense of vulnerability? The following steps can help.

Identifying your feelings

Naming the feelings you're experiencing can be difficult. For one thing, you may have trouble putting labels on your emotions. If so, consider the following terms for negative feelings—and work to develop your "feelings vocabulary":

Impatient	Frustrated
Annoyed	Jealous
Defensive	Afraid
Sad	Ashamed
Fearful	Vulnerable
Betrayed	Hurt
Confused	Isolated
Embarrassed	Self-conscious
Angry	Disappointed
Anxious	Worried
Skeptical	Bewildered
Lonely	Nervous

You may also have difficulty identifying your feelings if you tend to "hide" them in other comments during a prickly discussion with someone else. The table "Hiding your feelings" shows examples.

By expanding your feelings vocabulary and detecting unexpressed feelings and thoughts, you can more easily be fully present and responsible in a difficult interaction.

Hiding your feelings

If you said . . .	You may be . . .	And you may be feeling . . .
"The solution is for you to get these tasks done within budget."	Rushing to solve the problem	Fear that you won't get funding for a subsequent project
"You're unbelievably apathetic."	Characterizing the other person	Disappointed that the other person seems un-committed to the work
"You should have supported my proposal at the meeting."	Making judgments about how a peer is supposed to behave	Angry at a colleague who you thought backed your ideas
"Why did you ignore my memo about the new strategy?"	Making an attribution about someone else's intent	Worried about your leadership abilities

You can help the other person identify and describe his or her feelings as well. For example:

- **Explore hints.** "You mentioned an interest in being promoted. I wonder if you're angry because I got the project and you didn't."

- **Ask questions.** "What else might be bothering you about this situation?"

- **Offer observations.** "I notice that you're not looking me in the eye. Are you feeling embarrassed about how the presentation went?"

Reframing destructive thoughts

Difficult emotions and thoughts that trigger them are hard to bear. You don't have to carry them around like a backpack. With some self-empathy and reflection, you can experience and dissolve difficult feelings in relative short order. Consider these techniques:

- **Explore the other person's intentions and facts.** If you discover that your employee had good intentions and legitimate reasons when he decided not to show up at a weekly meeting, your annoyance may fade away.

- **Examine your contributions to the problem.** If you realize that you've advised employees to focus more on completing a project than on filling out paperwork, your frustration over late reports may lose its edge.

- **Ask what assumptions are causing your feelings.** If you find that your assumption that a colleague doesn't value product quality as much as you do is mistaken, you may feel less anger over her tendency to take quality-control shortcuts.

- **Feel and express your feelings.** One reason that feelings turn into a "state" or mood is that we simply don't feel and express them—to ourselves or others. When you're scared, it makes a lot of sense to say to yourself or a colleague, "I feel a bit worried about this assignment," and to have the other person simply witness and acknowledge your feeling, without having to change it.

Strategies for Transforming Angry Feelings into Productive Action

Anger can be one of the most intense and troubling emotions that come up during a conflict. The following strategies can help you manage anger effectively.

1. Recognize that you have a right to feel anger and to express it—constructively.

2. Commit to learning how to express anger constructively. Consider finding a coach who can help you.

3. Watch for signs that you're stuffing down angry feelings, such as the use of sarcasm, sniping, gossiping, or conspiring behind the other person's back.

4. Remember that the trigger to your anger is a behavior or situation—not another person.

5. Dispel intense anger through harmless physical activity, such as hitting a cushion for several minutes. Or channel it into productive routine activities, such as cleaning up your office. Or work through it with a trusted friend who can help you identify the causes of your anger rather than stir it up further.

6. Express anger constructively by describing your emotion to the person whose behaviors upset you, rather than making threats or accusations. For example, "When you missed two meetings in a row, I felt angry because other team members didn't get the information they needed to carry out their part of the project. I couldn't meet my need for integrity and effectiveness."

7. If you have trouble describing your anger to someone you work with, write down all the behaviors or situations that make you furious. Ask him or her to do the same. Get together to discuss the important items on your respective lists, taking turns and listening without interrupting.

Expressing feelings productively

After reframing destructive thoughts, name the feeling that you experience. Your goal is to express yourself honestly—without judging or blaming the other person.

Here's an example: "I'm not sure if this makes sense, but when you ignored my memo, I felt doubts about my ability to lead this team. Then I started worrying that the project would fail. I found myself getting frustrated over not being able to move the work forward."

Tip: To help dispel destructive thoughts and emotions during a difficult interaction, remind yourself of a humorous incident. You'll reduce your anxiety. Consider sharing the incident with the other party. You may ease their anxiety too. Humor promotes relaxation and openness to new ideas. Refrain from using inside jokes, cultural allusions, or jokes that make light of the other person's issues or concerns.

Step 3: Managing Threats to Your Self-Image

WHILE DISCUSSING DIFFICULT interactions with another person, you may begin worrying that your perceptions about yourself are called into question. For example, suppose a direct report says, "I didn't attend the meeting because I didn't think you valued my ideas." In response, you wonder to yourself, "Maybe I'm not a competent manager after all."

For many people, the sense that their self-image is being challenged creates anxiety. It's useful to address feelings about self-image—in yourself and the other person—during tough interactions. Why? Anxiety about self-image can overwhelm us, making it virtually impossible to converse productively about *any* subject.

Understanding the threat

Your self-image comes from many different assumptions that you've made about yourself. Here are just a few examples:

- "I'm an effective manager."
- "I'm a good person."
- "I care about my employees."
- "I'm committed to my company's success."
- "I'm loyal."

Not surprisingly, it's probably important to you to continue seeing yourself in these terms. After all, few people like to view themselves in a negative light—as incompetent, uncaring, or disloyal.

This self-image may help you meet a need for self-esteem, competence, and appreciation from others. These are important needs. You can't sacrifice them. But you can select appropriate strategies for meeting those needs and giving other people the chance to help you meet them.

"No one can make us feel inferior without our consent."
—Eleanor Roosevelt

Despite our desire to think of ourselves in positive terms, we often view our self-image from an either/or mind-set: "I'm either loyal or disloyal," "I'm either caring or uncaring," and so forth. The problem with this mind-set is that it makes us less able to tolerate criticism and constructive feedback from others.

For instance, if a colleague says, "I was really disappointed when you didn't support my proposal," you might conclude, "He thinks I'm not a good person," or "Maybe I'm not a loyal colleague." Thinking that you are "disloyal" or "bad" is pretty difficult, maybe intolerable. You may practice *denial* instead—and shoot back with something like, "I *did* support your proposal; I can't see how you'd say that!"

Other reactions to challenges for our well-constructed self-image include:

- **Burying the feelings** and resorting to generalizations, abstractions, and a detached manner: "Let's calm down and establish precise standard operating procedures here."

- **Striking back** at the other person defensively: "Are you calling me a *liar*?"

- **Refusing to face the disagreement** directly or to take a stand: "Oh, who knows what's going on here . . . Anyway, did you see Tom's article in the newsletter yesterday?"

These reactions have one thing in common: none of them enables you to listen to constructive feedback and make the changes needed to improve the way you interact with others.

Handling the threats

Several strategies can help you effectively handle challenges to your self-image during a difficult interaction. For one thing, you can work to *understand your self-image*. List the assumptions that influence your self-image. Ask yourself which of these assumptions evoke the strongest feelings. These are the assumptions that will most likely trigger a feeling of threat to your self-image if they're called into question during a disagreement. By anticipating that you might experience anxiety or defensiveness over these elements of your self-image, you may be better able to control those feelings if they do arise.

You can also *adopt a "both/and" mind-set.* Instead of assuming that you can be *either* competent *or* incompetent, remind yourself that you—and everyone else—are much more complex than that. Each person is a mix of positive and negative qualities, and no one is *always* anything. You're probably competent at some things and not so skilled at others. It's appropriate to feel good about many aspects of yourself and ambivalent about many others.

In addition, you can *accept imperfection.* Acknowledge that everyone makes mistakes at times. Everyone also has complicated motivations. For instance, perhaps you genuinely wanted to expedite a project by taking a delegated task back from an employee who couldn't seem to handle it. But deep down, you also knew that this action would let you communicate your frustration—without having to experience an uncomfortable discussion. So, you had admirable and not-so-admirable motives.

Finally, you can *find the need below the image.* Remember that you are human, and we humans have needs. Here are some basic needs that we have in the workplace.

Effectiveness	Appreciation
Integrity	Contribution
Safety	Enjoyment
Esteem	Meaning
Partnership	Movement
Creativity	Relaxation
Respect	Clarity

Helping others handle self-image threats

Just as you need to deal with perceived threats to your self-image during a confrontation, so does the other person. You can help him or her manage anxiety about self-image by raising the issue explicitly. For example:

- **Admit your own self-image concerns.** For example, "I tend to be sensitive to criticisms about my leadership style. But I know I need your feedback. So bear with me if I seem to be getting a bit defensive." By openly acknowledging your own anxieties about self-image, you may make it easier for the other person to do the same.

- **Ask questions about self-image.** For instance, "I'm sensing that this situation is about whether you're committed to this project. Is that how you're seeing it, too?"

- **View the other person as human, too.** Remind yourself that he or she makes mistakes and has complex motivations. Acknowledge in your own mind that the other person is neither completely competent nor utterly incompetent, neither totally caring about the project nor completely uncaring, and so forth.

- **Help others name the need that's not being met.** Take a guess at what's going on below the surface. For example, "Pat, I'm guessing that you really want to get this project completed by tomorrow, that you're a bit nervous about it, and that you've got a need for integrity here because you made a commitment to the team. Does that resonate with you?"

By acknowledging concerns about self-image and helping others deal with them, you can more easily discuss unproductive behaviors—and change them to improve the quality of your interactions.

Step 4: Solving the Real Problem

YOU'VE HAD SOME preliminary conversations with someone about the conflict plaguing your working relationship. And you've agreed that you want to improve things. Now it's time to conduct a conversation specifically geared to solving the problem. There are many ways to have this interaction. The approaches below will help you craft an enduring solution—rather than a one-time, temporary fix.

Framing the problem productively

As you discuss the difficulties between you and the other individual, keep framing the problem in productive ways. The table "Effective and ineffective framing" shows contrasting examples.

Sharing and listening

As you converse, continue sharing your viewpoint and listening, to understand the other person's perspective. Apply these practices:

- **Sharing.** Cite the experiences, motivations, and emotions that are influencing your perceptions of the problem. Reaffirm your commitment to improving the relationship. Make it clear that you view the other person as a partner in the process of addressing the difficulties between you.

- **Listening.** Ask questions to probe for more information from the other person about his or her experiences, motivations, emotions, and perceptions. Use paraphrasing to test your understanding of what you're hearing. Acknowledge the feelings behind any accusations or criticisms you hear.

Your goal in sharing and listening is to piece together a picture of how the two of you got into the difficult situation.

Effective and ineffective framing

Framing principle	What you might say	What not to say
Describe your difficulties as differences between you, not character flaws.	"Joan, it seems you've been emphasizing the importance of staying within budget on this project. I've been assuming that meeting the interim deadlines is our top priority."	"Joan, you don't seem to care about keeping this project on schedule. You keep missing the interim deadlines we've established."
Focus on perceptions, not presumed truths.	"Larry, to my mind, achieving the quality levels we've established means producing error-free reports."	"Larry, we've got to aim for zero mistakes in the reports we're producing. That's what quality is all about."
Emphasize contributions, not blame.	"Sarah, I've played my own part in this problem—by neglecting to let you know my priorities."	"Sarah, you're the one who didn't understand the importance of formatting the proposal in the right way."
Communicate feelings, not accusations.	"Peter, I feel frustrated when you don't do what you said you would do for the project team."	"Peter, you've really made me angry; you can't be relied on follow through with commitments."

Steps for Using Active Listening

1. **Listen to the other person.** Give the other person your full attention, resisting any urge to interrupt, plan your next comment, or
   judge the other person. Use nonverbal behavior—such as leaning
   forward and nodding—to demonstrate that you're really listening.

2. **Get the other person to clarify his or her position.** Ask open-
   ended questions to encourage the other person to clarify his or her
   position and interests regarding the issue that is at the heart of
   your conflict. Start your questions with phrases such as "Tell me
   about . . ." "Explain . . ." "How do you feel about . . ." "Describe . . ."
   "What happened when . . ."

3. **Paraphrase to show your understanding.** Periodically paraphrase
   what you're hearing, being sure to reflect the emotions as well as
   the content of the message. For example: "As I understand it, your
   position is . . ." or "You seem to be concerned about . . ." If the other
   person disagrees with your paraphrasing, ask him or her to clarify
   the point. Then paraphrase again to see whether you understand
   the message.

4. **Determine whether your interpretations are becoming more
   accurate.** As the discussion progresses, listen for signals that your
   interpretations of what you're hearing are becoming more accurate. Comments from the other person such as "That's exactly what
   I meant" and "That's right! I think you understand my problem" indicate that you've practiced good active listening. Body language
   such as smiling, nodding, and sighs of relief also suggest that you're
   on the right track.

"In the middle of every difficulty lies opportunity."
—Albert Einstein

Developing a plan for change

To craft an effective plan for change, explore potential solutions that satisfy each side's differing concerns and interests. For example, here's how Matt, a manager, resolved a difficulty with Brenda, a direct report:

Matt: We've had our ongoing differences about whether it's worth making these product demos. You know, I've never understood why it takes so long to get them out and why they're so expensive.

Brenda: Well, we want to get it right, so we consult with all the parties involved. We hold focus groups and then go through several rounds of review—sometimes up to five rounds. This is all so we can produce the best product demo possible.

Matt: Ah. I think we have different perceptions about what's critical. You're focusing on quality, which I understand. But I'm looking at the bottom line. I'd rather get a very good and cost-effective demo out in a timely manner than shoot for perfection.

Brenda: How good is "very good"?

Matt: Good enough for the customers to get a clear and compelling sense of the product . . . Let me ask you this: how valuable are the focus groups?

Brenda: That's hard to evaluate. People do disagree about their value. Sometimes we really need to find something out, and other times it's more standard routine.

Matt: And the reviews? When do you stop getting *critical* feedback and start getting feedback to, you know, change a single word or use a slightly different color?

Brenda: I'd say . . . round 4.

Matt: So, how about holding focus groups only when there's a clear need and cutting the number of reviews to three? Would we end up with a quality that you could feel comfortable with?

Brenda: Yes, I think I could live with that.

As with all action plans, you need to clarify how you'll carry out your plan for managing a difficult situation with another person. That way, you can help ensure that the solution you've developed resolves the problem you've identified. Keep these principles in mind as you discuss ways to implement the plan:

- **Determine how you'll measure success.** In Matt and Brenda's case, they might decide to measure progress by comparing the number of focus groups held for the current demo against the number held for previous demos—to ensure that fewer focus groups are held. They might also check whether the number of reviews is in fact cut down to three, as they agreed. And they might determine how to assess demo quality—for example, by the number of questions that customers have after using a demo.
- **Decide how you'll communicate going forward.** Will you meet once a week to discuss how things are going and make nec-

essary changes to the action plan? Will you check with each other daily by phone or e-mail? How will you handle any tension that arises during these discussions? Will you establish ground rules, such as "No blaming or character judgments allowed"?

Practical Steps to Improve How You Manage Difficult Interactions

1. **Document your difficult interactions.** Over a few weeks, keep track of difficult interactions you experience in the workplace. Record your observations in a notebook, indicating what caused each conflict, what happened during each situation, and what the outcome was.

2. **Identify patterns and explore your attitudes.** Analyze your observations to determine whether they form a pattern. For example, do you tend to avoid conflict as much as possible? Let the other person have his or her way all the time? Promote win-lose situations rather than win-win?

   Also think about your attitudes about difficult interactions. For instance, do you tend to assume that difficult situations are others' fault? Believe that you have no hope of improving a difficult situation? Believe that problems will resolve themselves? Fear interpersonal conflict?

3. **Prepare an improvement plan.** Identify ways to change unproductive attitudes toward difficult interactions. For example, remind yourself that most problems don't resolve themselves, and that you're not trying to change another person; you're attempting

to alter the way the two of you interact. To generate ideas for improving your ability to manage difficult interactions, talk with colleagues who are skilled at handling conflict, and read books on the subject. Consider getting coaching in conflict management.

Using what you've learned, define actions you'll take to strengthen your skills. For example, will you ask a colleague to help you role-play an interaction about a particular conflict with an employee? Take a course on conflict management? Try dealing with a relatively minor difficulty and then move on to more challenging situations?

4. **Implement your plan.** Carry out your plan, checking your progress at least once a week to ensure that you stay on track. Consider asking a trusted colleague to check in with you, to help ensure that you remain accountable for carrying out your plan.

5. **Assess your results.** Once you've carried out your plan, document another few weeks' worth of difficult interactions. Compare the results of your new style with those of your old style. Are you reaching more satisfactory agreements with fewer negative repercussions? Do you have more productive and realistic attitudes about difficult interactions? If not, move on to step 6.

6. **Make any necessary changes to your plan.** Determine why you did not get good results from your previous plan. For instance, did you practice new conflict-management skills with overly challenging situations first, instead of starting with more manageable difficulties? Using your insights, develop a revised plan for improving the way in which you manage difficult interactions. Carry out the plan and again assess your results, continuing to fine-tune your plan until you see positive results from your conflict-management style.

Helping Your Employees Manage Difficult Interactions

I T'S ALMOST ALWAYS best for your direct reports to resolve conflicts without your intervention. And it's useful for you to set that expectation with your direct reports. But how do you know when things have gone too far, and you need to step in?

Before we jump into this topic, note this important point: *if a conflict involves illegal conduct, such as sexual harassment or civil rights violations, it goes far beyond the definition of* difficult interaction. *In such cases, you need to consult the appropriate resources (typically your company's HR or legal department) to handle the situation.*

Deciding whether to intervene

When conflict arises among your employees, consider whether to play an active role in helping the parties involved resolve a dispute. As a manager, you can coach your direct reports so that they learn how to manage difficult interactions themselves.

In some cases you may also decide to intervene directly in a disagreement between your employees. Some experts suggest that if a dispute does not interfere with an employee's performance, does not disrupt the work environment, and doesn't violate company policy, then "benign neglect" may be your best approach. Not intervening gives your direct reports an opportunity to work out their difficult interactions on their own and meld into a high-performing unit, as well as strengthen their problem-solving skills. I tend to agree. In cases like that, I'll often simply ask, "How are things going on the ABC project?" and give the employee herself the opportunity to ask for coaching.

You *should* intervene when conflicts disrupt the work environment or hamper productivity. Intervention is also important when:

- A disagreement erupts between an assertive employee and a timid person, or the two individuals are of unequal rank.

- An argument between two direct reports has broadened to encompass additional staff members.

- The dispute has escalated into a series of personal attacks.

- One or both of the individuals involved asks for your assistance.

As noted above, if the situation involves illegal conduct, such as sexual harassment or civil rights violations, it's much more than a difficult interaction. Talk with someone in your company's HR or legal department about how to handle the situation.

Facilitating resolution

When you've identified a conflict between employees that merits your intervention, consider using the following process to facilitate resolution:

1. Help the individuals involved define the problem in specific, observable terms. Encourage them to describe the accompanying feelings, motivations, and needs.

What Would YOU Do?

Will Cooler Heads Prevail?

SABELLE, A MANAGER in a services firm, noticed an unpleasant situation developing between Bruce and Louisa, two members of her group. They indirectly criticized each other's competence during team meetings, and their subtle sniping had spilled over into a public e-mail exchange. Isabelle took stock of the facts. She suspected that the conflict was distracting them from doing their best work. Moreover, their comments were causing tension at meetings, upsetting the rest of the team, and threatening overall team performance. As a result, the work atmosphere was becoming decidedly nasty—not a good thing.

Isabelle set up a meeting for the three of them. She began by describing the destructive behaviors that Bruce and Louisa had been demonstrating. She also shared her concerns about the damage that their conflict was having on their own productivity, as well as the group's performance and morale. Bruce and Louisa immediately started defending their own positions—in increasingly heated language. Isabelle stopped them and asked them to take turns explaining the facts from their perspectives. Louisa went first. With her fists clenched, she complained: "It's so frustrating. I feel like I have to do Bruce's work for him when he doesn't hit his deadlines. I often end up staying late. He's not carrying his weight on the project." With mounting anger, Bruce quickly replied, "I've had it with this situation. I often have to redo my work because Louisa doesn't give me the information I need in advance. If she worked *with* me instead of *against* me, we could get the project work done on time—and done well."

Whoa, Isabelle thought to herself. *Things are getting out of hand.* She wondered how to get the meeting back on a productive track.

What would YOU do? The mentor will suggest a solution in *What You COULD Do.*

2. Ensure that each person listens carefully to the other. Model paraphrasing and other active-listening skills to demonstrate how this is done.

3. Help them identify areas of agreement. For example, perhaps both people do have a project's best interests at heart, but they have different views about how best to carry out the work.

4. Encourage the two individuals to brainstorm alternative solutions. Evaluate how well the proposed solutions satisfy their concerns and issues.

5. Suggest that the two create a problem-resolution plan. Help them create and get started implementing the plan if necessary.

6. Schedule future meetings during which the individuals involved will discuss, under your guidance, how things are going and whether the solution is working.

Coaching employees to improve their skills

To teach your direct reports to handle their conflicts themselves, consider implementing these coaching strategies:

- **Role-play conflict-resolution situations with one or more employees.** Ask employees for their opinions about what went well, what didn't go well, and how they might handle the next practice scenario better.

- **Establish goals for practicing and strengthening conflict-resolution skills.** For example, suggest that an employee identify a colleague with whom he or she has a fairly minor disagreement. The employee could practice conflict-management skills—such as framing the problem in terms of differences and expressing emotions instead of blaming—with this "safe" person. He or she could then gradually practice with more difficult situations.

- **Define ways to measure progress toward goals.** For instance, will your direct report have achieved the goal if he or she conducts three interactions with a colleague that lead to improvements in the relationship?

- **Provide needed resources, such as access to conflict-resolution courses or workshops.** Suggest that the employee talk about conflict resolution with individuals whom you know to be particularly skilled.

While coaching, keep in mind that your employees will need time to fully grasp the art of managing difficult interactions.

What You COULD Do.

Remember Isabelle's concern about how to handle Bruce and Louisa's frustration?

Here's what the mentor suggests:

At this point in the meeting, Isabelle needs to help Bruce and Louisa acknowledge and address the powerful emotions that have arisen. Now that she has listened intently to her two employees as they individually presented the so-called facts (as *they* saw them), she can summarize what she's hearing: "I can see that each of you is extremely frustrated. But notice that you each mentioned the project and obviously want it to succeed. You both have high standards and feel strongly about not letting those standards slip. Let's concentrate on that." The emotional intensity in the room would probably begin to drop as Bruce and Louisa started focusing on their shared interests in standards and the project, rather than their frustrations with each other.

Before the meeting, Bruce and Louisa had expressed their emotions indirectly through sniping at one another. Each felt attacked—so they went on the attack. As the old adage goes, "The best defense is a good offense." During the meeting, Isabelle started breaking that cycle by first allowing Bruce and Louisa to express their viewpoints. She can further break the cycle by focusing the discussion on their shared priorities.

They'll also need frequent opportunities to hone their skills. Some individuals may not even initially be aware that they lack the ability to skillfully handle conflict. Others may know they need to strengthen these skills but don't know how to do so. Still others may understand the techniques behind managing difficult interactions but need to stop and think before applying them. All of these individuals could benefit from your guidance. With enough coaching, practice, and feedback, your direct reports should eventually be able to manage their own disagreements effectively.

Consider the difficult interactions currently cropping up among your employees. In which ones should you intervene? Which ones should be resolved by the people involved? How might you coach your direct reports so that they learn how to manage difficult interactions themselves?

Tips and Tools

Tools for
Managing Difficult
Interactions

Finding the Source of the Difficulty

Use this worksheet to help you isolate the sources of difficult interactions you're experiencing with someone at work.

How does your perception of the situation differ from the other person's?

How might the other person's motivations differ from yours?

What do you find difficult about the other person's work style?

What do you find difficult about the other person's communication style?

Describe the issue at hand. What are your and the other person's positions and interests regarding this issue?

What experiential, cultural, or other differences may be contributing to the problem?

Bottom line—what conclusions can you draw about the source of the difficulty?

Deciding Whether to Deal with a Difficult Interaction

*Use this worksheet to determine whether you should manage
a difficult interaction or let it go.*

How would you characterize the importance of your relationship with this person?

How will the difficult situation affect your ability to work with this person in the future?
(Use a scale of 1–5, with 5 being the greatest impact)

Not at all ──────────────────────────────────── Tremendously
☐ 1 ☐ 2 ☐ 3 ☐ 4 ☐ 5

If the two of you could successfully address the conflict, how much would it benefit your
working relationship?
(Use a scale of 1–5, with 5 being the greatest potential)

No benefit ──────────────────────────────────── Enormous benefit
☐ 1 ☐ 2 ☐ 3 ☐ 4 ☐ 5

How high are the stakes in your relationship with this person?

☐ High   ☐ Medium   ☐ Low

Is your relationship with this person short term or long term?

☐ Short   ☐ Long

How likely is it that the relationship could be improved? *(If one or both parties have deep
emotional problems or a history of destructive behaviors with a wide range of people in many
different situations, the relationship probably can't be improved.)*
(Use a scale of 1–5, with 5 being most likely)

Not likely at all ──────────────────────────────── Very likely
☐ 1 ☐ 2 ☐ 3 ☐ 4 ☐ 5

What are the potential costs of addressing this difficult situation?

What are the potential benefits of addressing the situation?

Is the payoff worth the time commitment?

☐ Yes   ☐ No

Assessing Perceptions and Behavior During a Difficult Interaction

Use this assessment to define a difficult interaction from your perspective as well as from the other person's perspective.

What is the situation?

What is your perception of the situation?

What experiences, information, motivations, interests, and assumptions are causing you to see the situation that way?

How does the other person see the situation?

What experiences, information, motivations, interests, and assumptions are causing the other person to see the situation that way?

Summarize the major differences between the two sides' views of the difficult situation. For each difference, list possible resolutions or areas of common ground.

Difference	Resolution/Common Ground

Discussing a Difficult Interaction

Use this tool to assess how effectively you've discussed a difficult interaction with the other person involved. For each statement, indicate "yes" or "no."

During one or more interactions, the other person and I have ...	Yes	No
1. Discussed our differing interests in the issue at hand.		
2. Acknowledged other differences, such as work or communication styles, motivations, perceptions about what's critical, and experiential and cultural backgrounds.		
3. Agreed that we want to improve matters between us.		
4. Shared our impressions of what's going on and the reasons behind our impressions.		
5. Described the feelings we're experiencing as a result of our difficulties.		
6. Acknowledged concerns about self-image and meeting underlying needs that have cropped up because of the conflict.		
7. Acknowledged that no one is perfect and that everyone makes mistakes.		
8. Demonstrated active listening with one another—for instance, by asking questions, paraphrasing, and not interrupting.		
9. Resisted the urge to blame, accuse, or judge one another.		
10. Stated our individual contributions to the problem.		
11. Found ways to defuse intense emotions—for example, by taking breaks and then returning to the discussion.		
12. Framed the discussion in terms of differences, not character flaws.		
13. Focused on differing perceptions, not presumed truths.		
14. Worked to identify emotions hidden behind any accusations or judgments.		
15. Worked to remove barriers to our ability to deal with the difficulty—such as fear of conflict or the belief that the problem will resolve itself.		
On the basis of your responses, how effective would you say your interactions about the difficult interaction with the other person have been?		

Consider the statements to which you responded "no." What actions might you take in a subsequent interaction with this person to improve your skills at managing the difficulty?

Creating a Plan for Change

*Use this worksheet to create a plan for addressing difficult
interactions with a particular person at work.*

1. Describe the difficult situation.

2. List the differences (in motivations, interests, work styles, and so forth) that have led to the conflict.

3. List the potential solutions to the problem that you and the other person have discussed. Ask how well each proposed solution would satisfy both parties' concerns and interests, even if partially.

4. Select the one best solution.

5. Clarify how you'll implement the selected solution.

6. Explain how you'll measure success. (How will you and the other person know that the difficulty between you has been resolved?)

7. Define ground rules for implementing the plan—for example, "Notify the other person several days ahead of time if we can't make a scheduled meeting or discussion."

8. Clarify how you'll communicate going forward. (Will you and the other person meet weekly to discuss progress on the plan? Will you check in with each other by e-mail periodically?)

9. Describe how you'll handle tensions or backsliding while implementing the plan, and how you'll go about making needed revisions to the plan.

Resolving a Difficult Interaction Between Employees

Use this worksheet to identify interemployee conflicts that merit intervention, to facilitate productive interactions between the individuals involved, and to identify strategies for coaching employees on better managing their difficult interactions.

Part I. Deciding Whether to Intervene

Statement	Yes	No
1. The conflict is between an assertive employee and a timid person.		
2. The conflict is between two people of different rank.		
3. The conflict has broadened beyond the two people to encompass additional staff members.		
4. The conflict involves illegal conduct, such as sexual harassment or civil rights violations.		
5. The individuals involved aren't aware that their difficulties are causing problems with productivity.		
6. The individuals involved are aware that their difficulties are causing problems, but they lack the ability to manage the difficulty themselves.		

If you answered "yes" to any of the above statements, you'll need to intervene in the problem. Proceed to part II.

Part II. Identifying People with Required Skills

Date of interaction:

Participants:

Participant 1's view of the problem (include feelings, motivations, interests, and underlying needs):

continued

Participant 2's view of the problem (include feelings, motivations, interests, and underlying needs):

Areas of agreement:

Potential solutions (list how each alternative satisfies the disputants' concerns and issues):

Problem-resolution plan:

Future meetings to check progress:

Part III. Coaching Employees in Conflict Resolution

Helping your employees to resolve a conflict is useful, but teaching them to manage difficult interactions themselves is even more useful. Below, identify how you will coach your direct reports to better handle difficult interactions themselves.

Employee	Coaching Strategy

Test Yourself

This section offers ten multiple-choice questions to help you identify your baseline knowledge of the essentials of managing difficult interactions. Answers to the questions are given at the end of the test.

1. Difficult interactions may escalate to highly undesirable outcomes in the form of strained relationships, wasted time, and declining performance. Two of the three statements below are also true about these difficult interactions. Which is the *false* statement?

  a. Many people feel reluctant to deal with confrontations.
  b. Not all confrontations are worth the time and energy required to manage them.
  c. Over time, the majority of confrontations resolve themselves.

2. Many managers avoid dealing with conflict because they fear worsening the situation. Which of the following strategies would you use to overcome fear of conflict?

  a. Acknowledge that conflict is part of life, and focus on the positive outcomes of addressing conflict.
  b. Acknowledge that you've played a role in the problem situation that has come up between you and the other person.
  c. Identify actions you can take to begin improving the tough situation at hand.

3. What is the primary cause behind most difficult interactions in the workplace?

   a. One person's malicious intent toward another.

   b. An individual's poor character or incompetence.

   c. Differences between people.

4. Some disagreements arise because the people involved take different positions on an issue or have different interests regarding that issue. What are "interests"?

   a. A person's stance on a particular issue.

   b. A person's underlying desire or need regarding a particular issue.

   c. A person's plans for resolving a particular issue.

5. Your time and energy are limited, so you need to carefully evaluate which difficult interactions merit your attention and which should be let go. In which situation might you decide to try to resolve a particular series of conflicts with someone at work?

   a. You've noticed that the other person has a long history of troubled relationships with many people across a wide range of situations.

   b. You've learned that the other person is profoundly troubled emotionally.

   c. Your relationship with that person is long term, and the stakes are high.

6. While discussing conflicts with the other person involved, you need to uncover the facts of the situation—or what's really going on. Which of the following statements is true about this process?

   a. Each person's experiences, assumptions about what's important, and intentions will influence his or her perception of the facts.

   b. Each person in the conflict will have similar perceptions about what's going on that has led to the difficult situation.

   c. One person is likely to have made a significantly larger contribution to the problem than the other person has made.

7. In addition to understanding each person's perceptions about what's going on in a difficult interaction, it's important to identify the emotions involved. Which of the following statements is true about the process of identifying emotions?

   a. Some managers have trouble putting labels on their emotions and need to develop their "feelings vocabulary."

   b. When a person experiences an emotion during a difficult interaction, he or she cannot change that emotion.

   c. In describing your emotions during a conflict, you should focus on the most intense feeling only.

8. In addition to understanding each person's perceptions of what's going on and identifying the emotions raised by a difficult interaction, the individuals involved must address concerns about self-image. Which of the following statements most strongly suggests that the speaker has self-image concerns?

- a. "I really made a serious mistake that day, when I forgot to tell Jorge how important that meeting was."
- b. "I've failed to communicate my expectations clearly enough to Maya. I'm not a good manager."
- c. "I've got to be more open to negative feedback about my performance in this new role."

9. During a recent interaction, James and Carla—a manager and an employee on a prototype-development team—realized they had conflicting perceptions about what's critical. The two worked out a solution to their conflict that entails changing the number of prototype iterations conducted. After implementing their plan, James and Carla will compare the number of iterations conducted for the current set of prototypes to the number they agreed to in their plan. But they've left out a step that's crucial for successful implementation of their plan. What is it?

- a. Piecing together a picture of how they got into their difficult situation.
- b. Selecting metrics to assess how well they've carried out their solution.
- c. Deciding how they'll communicate going forward.

10. When two of your employees get embroiled in a conflict, you have to determine whether to intervene. Which of the following conditions would warrant intervention?

a. The problem has erupted between two employees who have equal standing and rank in your department or team.

b. You've determined that the confrontation has begun encompassing additional staff members beyond the original disputants.

c. You've determined that the situation doesn't involve possible civil rights violations or other potentially illegal conduct.

Answers to test questions

1, c. Most difficult interactions don't in fact resolve themselves. Time seldom resolves problems—people do.

2, a. The first step in overcoming fear of conflict is to acknowledge that while conflict can feel uncomfortable, it is also a part of life. Focusing on the potential positive outcomes of addressing conflict—and identifying ways to become more comfortable facing conflict—can help you move past your fear.

3, c. Most difficult interactions in the workplace stem from differences between people—in interests, motivations, perceptions, work and communication styles, and life experiences or cultural background.

4, b. Interests are a person's desires regarding a particular issue. For example, a new team member who wants to receive as much vacation time as other team members receive (his *position* on the *issue* of vacation time) may have an *interest* in being treated fairly—that is, a desire. Often, identifying differing interests can help the people involved to design creative solutions that satisfy both their interests.

5, c. When a particular workplace relationship is crucial and you need to collaborate with that person for a long time under high-stakes conditions, you'll want to find ways to manage difficult interactions with that person. By contrast, if you have a troubled interaction with a colleague on a short-term, minor, and one-time project, you probably won't want to invest the time and energy in trying to improve the relationship.

6, a. There are two sides to every story, and each person views a conflict according to a set of facts that he or she perceives. Both people in a conflict might be using a different set of facts to form an impression of what's going on. For example, if Harry experienced problems on an earlier project because of late updates, he might argue, "Mary is jeopardizing our project by not submitting updates on time." Harry believes that not following through on paperwork results in failure. Mary, meanwhile, saw an earlier project fall apart because people spent too much time on paperwork. Both people's experiences are true for them—and influence their view of the facts.

7, a. By developing a "feelings vocabulary," a manager can more accurately describe the emotions that he or she is experiencing during a confrontation. The manager can also better understand the other person's descriptions of emotions.

8, b. Concerns about self-image can crop up during a difficult interaction if a person has an either-or mind-set: "I'm either loyal or disloyal," "I'm either competent or incompetent," and so forth. This mind-set makes it impossible to tolerate criticism from others or to acknowledge that one has contributed to a problem—two abilities that are essential to managing conflicts. Thus it's vital to acknowledge and address self-image concerns while discussing difficult interactions.

9, c. James and Carla don't seem to have determined how they'll communicate going forward—including how they'll discuss progress on their plan, handle tensions that arise during these discussions, and make necessary changes to their plan. Like the other steps they've taken (clarifying the differences behind their difficulty and selecting metrics for assessing the success of their plan), this step is essential for ensuring successful implementation of any solution to a difficult interaction.

10, b. When a conflict starts encompassing additional staff members beyond the original disputants, it's best to intervene. You can facilitate resolution of a confrontation by helping the disputants define the problem in specific terms, listen to one another, identify areas of agreement, and implement solutions that satisfy the disputants' differing concerns and issues. You can also use coaching to teach employees to manage their difficult interactions on their own rather than pulling other people into their disputes.

To Learn More

Articles

Craumer, Martha. "Confrontation Without Conflict." *Harvard Management Communication Letter* (June 2002).

> Most of us are reluctant to confront a colleague about behavior that is distracting, unprofessional, or just plain rude. But avoiding the problem can affect morale and productivity. This article explains how to defuse potential workplace conflicts while they're still manageable, and includes a sidebar on how to approach a difficult interaction.

Gary, Loren. "Becoming a Resonant Leader." *Harvard Management Update* (July 2002).

> After the events of 2001, leaders are being asked to act with greater integrity and to be more emotionally available to their employees. Leaders need to learn to adapt to this new work environment, using such tools as emotional intelligence, and to hone their ability to handle the emotional turbulence that comes with adaptive change.

Hackley, Susan. "When Life Gives You Lemons: How to Deal with Difficult People." *Negotiation* (November 2004).

> As William Ury, author of *Getting Past No: Negotiating with Difficult People*, explains, we all have to negotiate at times with

difficult people. They might be stubborn, arrogant, hostile, greedy, or dishonest. Or they might be, for the most part, affable. But even ordinarily reasonable people can turn into opponents. For instance, your boss can be collaborative and understanding most of the time, but make unreasonable demands on a Friday afternoon. Learn how to turn your angst into approbation and get past "no."

Harvard Business School Publishing. "Leading by Feel." *Harvard Business Review* (January 2004).

Empathy, intuition, and self-awareness are essential to good leadership, but they can be tricky to hone and dangerous to use. In this article, eighteen leaders and scholars explore how to manage emotional intelligence.

Weeks, Holly. "Taking the Stress Out of Stressful Interactions." *Harvard Business Review* OnPoint Enhanced Edition (March 2002).

Stressful interactions are unavoidable in life. In business, they can run the gamut from firing a subordinate to, curiously enough, receiving praise. But whatever the context, stressful interactions carry a heavy emotional load. Indeed, they cause such anxiety that most people simply avoid them. Yet it can be extremely costly to dodge issues, appease difficult people, and smooth over antagonisms; avoidance usually only worsens a problem or a relationship. Using vivid examples of the three basic stressful interactions that people bump up against most often in the workplace, the author explains how managers can improve those interactions unilaterally. To begin with, they should approach the situations with greater self-awareness.

Awareness building is not about endless self-analysis; much of it simply involves making tacit knowledge about oneself more explicit. Knowing how you react in a stressful situation will teach you a lot about your trouble areas and can help you master stressful situations.

Weiss, Jeff, and Jonathan Hughes. "Want Collaboration? Accept—and Actively Manage—Conflict." *Harvard Business Review* (March 2005).

The fact is, you can't improve collaboration until you've addressed the issue of conflict. The authors offer six strategies for effectively managing conflict: devise and implement a common method for resolving conflict; provide people with criteria for making trade-offs; use the escalation of conflict as an opportunity for coaching; establish and enforce a requirement of joint escalation; ensure that managers resolve escalated conflicts directly with their counterparts; and make the process for escalated conflict resolution transparent. The first three strategies focus on the point of conflict; the second three focus on escalation of conflict up the management chain.

Books

Goleman, Daniel, Richard Boyatzis, and Annie McKee. *Primal Leadership: Learning to Lead with Emotional Intelligence.* Boston: Harvard Business School Press, 2004.

Drawing from decades of research within world-class organizations, the authors show that great leaders excel not just through skill and smarts, but by connecting with others using emotional intelligence (EI) competencies such as empathy and self-awareness.

Harvard Business School Publishing. *Dealing with Difficult People.* The Results-Driven Manager Series. Boston: Harvard Business School Press, 2004.

Concise, action-oriented, and packed with invaluable strategies and tools, this guide will help managers hone and polish skills for dealing with difficult people: avoiding conflicts and negativity, fostering positive behavior, and motivating underperformers.

Harvard Business School Publishing. *Harvard Business Review Management Dilemmas: When Good People Behave Badly*. Boston: Harvard Business School Press, 2004.

What would you do if one of your star performers mistreated other workers; your best manager "lost it" and humiliated a colleague in public; or a coworker began to exhibit strange, even frightening, behavior? This guide explores ways to handle a wide range of complex behavioral issues that affect employees and managers.

Rosenberg, Marshall B. *Nonviolent Communication: A Language of Life*. Puddledancer Press, Encinitas, CA, 2005.

This book is a practical toolkit for helping people speak and listen to each other as allies, not adversaries. Rosenberg, a psychiarist, describes how we have grown up in a culture of violent and defensive communication, and that we can get back to what we truly want—connection—by learning the language of feelings and needs. This book is a both a call for nonviolence and a step-by-step guide along the path to caring for ourselves and each other as human beings.

eLearning Programs

Harvard Business School Publishing. *Coaching for Results*. Boston: Harvard Business School Publishing, 2000.

Understand and practice how to effectively coach others by mastering the five core skills necessary for successful coaching:

- Observing
- Questioning
- Listening
- Feedback
- Agreement

Through interactive role-playing, expert guidance, and activities for immediate application at work, this program helps you coach successfully by preparing, discussing, and following up in any situation.

Harvard Business School Publishing. *Managing Difficult Interactions*. Boston: Harvard Business School Publishing, 2001.

This program will help you understand why disagreements occur and help you build conclusions collaboratively. These productive dialogue skills will lead to a more accurate, shared understanding of the information exchanged in your daily interactions. *Managing Difficult Interactions* examines techniques for approaching and handling difficult business interactions. The program explores how mental models influence our private thinking and, thus, our behavior. It presents the Left-Hand Column exercise as a technique for unveiling and examining our internal thought process. It also examines five unproductive thinking habits that many people fall into during difficult interactions, and offers five productive alternative ways of thinking. By examining your own thinking habits and actively seeking more productive mind-sets, you can learn to approach difficult interactions with confidence, avoid blaming, overcome defensiveness, and make better business decisions.

Harvard Business School Publishing. *Productive Business Dialogue.* Boston: Harvard Business School Publishing, 2002.

This program shows managers how to craft interactions that are fact based, minimize defensiveness, and draw out the best thinking from everyone involved. *Productive Business Dialogue* introduces the Ladder of Inference, a tool that helps participants in a dialogue understand the distinctions among fact, interpretation, and conclusions; and how making these distinctions clear can dramatically enhance the productivity of meetings and discussions. Through interactive, real-world scenarios, you will practice shaping interactions that maximize learning and lead to better-informed decisions.

Sources for Managing Difficult Interactions

The following sources aided in development of this topic:

Alessandra, Tony, and Michael J. O'Connor, with Janice Van Dyke. *People Smarts: Bending the Golden Rule to Give Others What They Want.* San Francisco, CA: Jossey-Bass, 1994.

Brinkman, Rick, with Rick Kirschner. *Dealing with People You Can't Stand: How to Bring Out the Best in People at Their Worst.* New York: McGraw-Hill, 1994.

Cava, Roberta. *Difficult People: How to Deal with Impossible Clients, Bosses and Employees.* Toronto: Key Porter Books Limited, 1990.

Delpo, Amy, and Lisa Guerin. *Dealing with Problem Employees: A Legal Guide.* Berkeley, CA: Nolo Press, 2001.

Friedman, Paul. *How to Deal with Difficult People.* Mission, KS: SkillPath Publications, 1994.

Harvard Business School Publishing. *Face-to-Face Communications for Clarity and Impact.* The Results-Driven Manager Series. Boston: Harvard Business School Press, 2004.

Interaction Associates. "Essential Facilitation." A four-day intensive workshop taught in cities across the United States.

Interaction Associates. "Facilitative Leadership: Tapping the Power of Participation." A three-day workshop taught in cities across the United States.

Interaction Associates. "Mastering Meetings." A two-day workshop taught in cities across the United States.

Personnel Decisions. *Successful Manager's Handbook: Development Suggestions for Today's Managers*. Edina, MN: Personnel Decisions International, 1992.

Stone, Douglas, Bruce Patton, and Sheila Heen. *Difficult Interactions: How to Discuss What Matters Most*. New York: Penguin Books, 1999.

Whitemyer, David. "Don't Just Do Something—Sit There." *Harvard Management Update* (December 2002).

Notes

How to Order

Harvard Business Press publications are available worldwide from your local bookseller or online retailer.

You can also call:
1-800-668-6780

Our product consultants are available to help you 8:00 a.m.–6:00 p.m., Monday–Friday, Eastern Time. Outside the U.S. and Canada, call: 617-783-7450.

Please call about special discounts for quantities greater than ten.

You can order online at:
www.HBSPress.org